THE WORLD'S
GREATEST PAINTINGS

THE WORLD'S GREATEST PAINTINGS

*Selected Masterpieces
of Famous Art Galleries*

EDITED BY
T. LEMAN HARE

ODHAMS PRESS LTD.
LONG ACRE, LONDON, W.C.2

FOREWORD

THIS work will be published in three volumes containing, in all, one hundred fine colour plates of well-known pictures from many lands. Perhaps I may explain that the purpose of these volumes is to place within the reach of a wide public, in addition to the plates, a brief account of the life and times of each master whose work is represented; avoiding, as far as possible, all discussion of technical matters in which that public will have little concern. No attempt can be made, even in one hundred reproductions, to do more than give typical examples of each master and period, neither is it claimed that in every case the " best work" of each painter has been included—that would lead to endless discussion—nor can one expect to find every great master represented, since that would require many more volumes.

There is so much nonsense spoken and written about Art to-day that the average man is, very naturally, inclined to be shy of the whole subject and suspicious of those who practise the Arts. He thinks, if this mass of contradiction and confusing jargon is the result of the love of Art, he had better do without Art altogether. There is no mystery about Art—but there is mystification without end evolved by certain critics who love to pose as superior persons. Such writers put forward the theory that the enjoyment of the Fine Arts is reserved for a select and exclusive minority, meaning, of course, themselves and their disciples. No greater error could be propounded than this which is a comparatively modern fallacy, and one which is so dangerous that if persisted in must in time bring into contempt everything and everyone connected with Art.

No great art—nor any great religion—can be above the heads of ordinary people for, if it be so, it has failed in its mission. You will certainly see in the pages which follow that the great painters of the past made no attempt to confuse or mystify those for whom they wrought their masterpieces. We cannot think of those who built our great English Cathedrals, and carved the decorations from solid stone, as men who would babble on the theories of their craft, and we know that they did not—and happily could not—write on them.

You will notice in the pictures which follow a consistent treatment and rendering by each artist of the atmosphere of his own time, and, in our day, it is useless to go back to ancient Greece, or elsewhere, in imitation of a Past, which *is* past—and it may be added that it is equally undesirable to practise an Art in an obscure way and explain its absurdity by saying it is "Futurist"!

And so you will see this rule has been followed by artists of widely different times and countries of rendering their own period. The Italian painters of the fifteenth and sixteenth centuries, for example, when at work on biblical subjects, always took as their models living persons, clothed them in their every-day costumes, and placed them in backgrounds of beautiful Italian landscapes. Again, in the French school—not much concerned perhaps with religious topics—you will notice each generation of painters is interested very much in his own times and above all in France herself, her people, customs, and scenery. In the famous Dutch school of the seventeenth century—with its delightful studies of home interiors, where the sunlight streams through the lofty windows—no attempt is made to seek subjects or models belonging to any other time or country.

These considerations may cause us to doubt whether some kind of modern art, having no hint of our time or country in it, can hope to interest future generations. In trying to get a correct understanding of what are called " Old Masters," we should do well to remember that the aim of each generation of painters in Italy was to make an advance, at least in technique, beyond the achievement of their predecessors. It is often felt by the average person that certain old works are puzzling, probably because they do not realise that a man can only work with the vision, manner, and materials of his own day; therefore it is unreasonable to demand, for example, perfect drawing and perspective from an artist who lived before the laws of perspective were discovered ! It is important also to avoid the tyranny of names, so we must not be induced to admire every picture merely because it was painted by a great master. There have been no infallible masters at any time, and naturally all the greatest men had their early periods, when they had not gained full experience. Again, there is that dreadful " off day " to consider, which afflicts, as we know, even the great cricketer—artist of the bat—so that he will be in good form to-day and not to-morrow. It is related of a great French painter that he calmly threw out of his studio window his many pictures which he judged had not " come off " and you may find it an interesting task to detect the good and bad days of great artists, and will be amused to note that the greatest men, when blessed with health, were doing their best work when very old in years.

Here, then, is the First Volume, with thirty-four superb examples of great paintings from public galleries and private collections in all parts of the world. In introducing these masterpieces, it is the sincere wish of the Editor and publisher that through the medium of these reproductions some of the charm and beauty of the originals may gladden the hearts and homes of a public who would otherwise be unable to see more than a few of the pictures that form this collection.

T. L. H.

CONTENTS

THE VISITATION

By MARIOTTO ALBERTINELLI

In the Uffizi Gallery—Florentine School

Mariotto Albertinelli
1474-1515

THE city of Florence, at the time of the birth of Mariotto Albertinelli, in 1474, although the centre of great artistic activity, was also a hot bed of civil and religious dispute, for the great Dominican Savonarola was at the height of his campaign against the secular and religious authorities, which was to end with his own death.

The story of Albertinelli is one of the strangest episodes of the period, on account of his lifelong and loyal friendship with his fellow-artist, a simple and gentle monk, Fra Bartolommeo, the inventor of the studio lay figure and a painter of rare quality, with a strong instinct for the large composition.

Nothing could be more opposed than the character of these two men; the one a timid, lovable religious, and the other a swaggering, noisy partisan and notoriously loose liver. So closely, however, did these two work together and resemble each other in their work that their pictures have been often attributed to each other. It seems certain, too, that when, in 1498, Fra Bartolommeo, on the death of Savonarola, retired to a monastery for the rest of his life, Albertinelli completed many of his unfinished works, a task no doubt congenial to him and one for which he was well equipped.

The picture here reproduced—"The Visitation," in the Uffizi, Florence, commissioned in 1503 by the congregation of Saints Martino and Elizabetta —is undoubtedly the master work of Albertinelli. It does not require much knowledge of Art to recognize, in this stately and beautiful composition, the work of a great master, though it may puzzle us, in view of what has been said as to the painter's character, to observe also the genuine, tender, and religious feeling which pervades it, and the simplicity of the composition.

It is related by Vasari that on one occasion this tempestuous painter, enraged by criticism upon his work, threw up his painting and retired, not to a monastery like his gentle friend, but to an inn which he kept for some years. His wild career ended at the early age of 41, in 1515.

The principal works of Albertinelli are in the leading galleries of Europe, but for beauty both of design and colour none compare with "The Visitation."

Edwin Austin Abbey, R.A.
1852-1911

THE painter of " O Mistress Mine" was the first of Shakespearean illustrators of his time. His beautiful drawings for the " Comedies " (with commentary by Swinburne) were an eagerly awaited feature of *Harper's Magazine* in the 'nineties, and were afterwards published in four volumes. It was whilst reading " Twelfth Night," that play which begins so enchantingly with Duke Orsino's invocation to music and love, that Abbey stumbled on the idea of this picture, not as relevant to the play, since it illustrates no part of it. But it is typical of Shakespeare's prodigality that he has put his exquisite song into the mouth of a clown, to be sung at the instigation of buffoons. Abbey seized upon its sheer beauty of sentiment as a pretext for devising this charming love-scene in which we see the anxious and desolated lover in the act of reclaiming his lost mistress. He is followed by his faithful troubadour who endeavours, by the strains of his lute, to awaken impassioned memories. " *O Mistress Mine where art thou roaming ?* "

It is clear that some disharmony has interrupted the course of true love, and that she, fearing for the future, has strayed from her adorer. There is a look of doubt upon her face, though she half relents, she hesitates to respond to his appeal. She looks at him from a distance, trying to stop her ears and, with the hand that he clasps, even seeks to push him from her. Perhaps she thinks of another lover. Let us hope that for them the song's message is the true one, " Journey's end in lovers' meeting."

Abbey revelled in his wardrobe. He had acquired a vast collection of Shakespearean and historical costumes and was happy in painting rich and voluminous draperies. He had a marked predilection for reds, purples, and lilacs, and indeed for all things fresh and bright in colour. The lady in the picture is clothed in rich habiliments (singularly unsuited, we may observe, for hasty flight or travel). After the picture was hung on the Academy walls, Abbey repainted entirely the lining of the sleeves. The study for the pergola and background was made at Ravello in Italy, in 1891. The place so enthralled the painter that he wrote to a friend, " a lovelier place than this . . . ain't ! "

O MISTRESS MINE

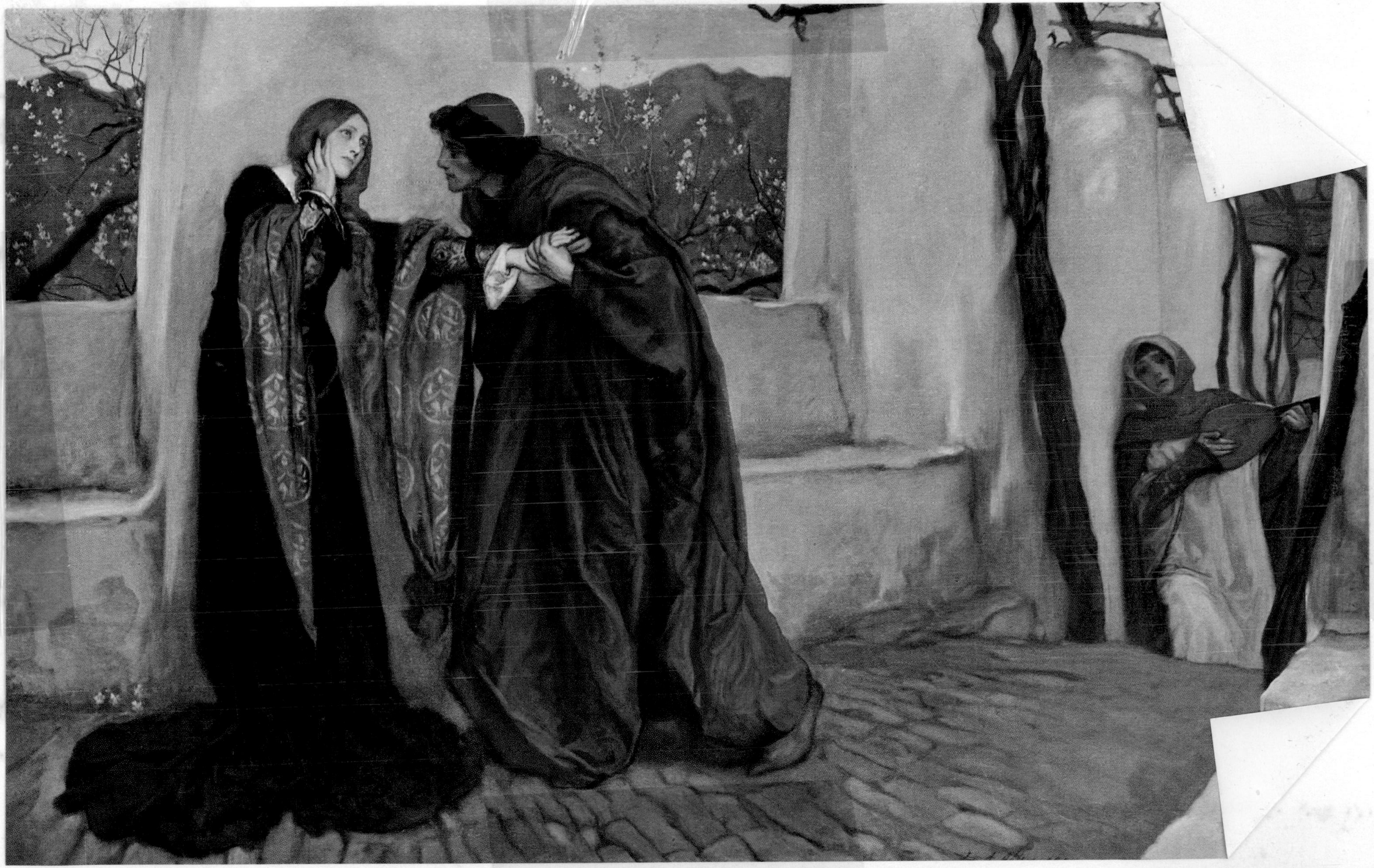

THE DOGE

By GIOVANNI BELLINI

In the National Gallery—Venetian School

Giovanni Bellini

1430-1516

THE Italian painters, as a whole, have been justly famous for their use of fine colour, but, as compared with the other schools of Italy, that of Venice stood out above all contemporaries on account of its instinctive feeling for brilliant colour and the superb manner in which it was used.

From very early times, the Church realized the importance of reaching the minds of the people, who could neither read nor write, by means of music and colour, so it came about that the leading artists were encouraged to decorate Church interiors with Biblical narrative, first of all with Mosaics composed of small pieces of coloured glass, or stone, inlaid, later on, by frescoes, or wall painting, and finally by tempera or oil paintings for altar pieces.

Giovanni Bellini was undoubtedly the greatest religious master of the fifteenth century at work in Venice, and it is interesting to note the large number of his pupils whose names came to be reckoned among the great painters of Italy.

About the year 1504 Giovanni Bellini painted a series of State portraits of the Doges of Venice, probably four. But the only one known to be still in existence is the magnificent portrait of Doge Leonardo Loredano in his State robes (here illustrated) which is, without the least doubt, one of the gems of the National Gallery collection. This portrait of the Doge (or Duke) of the Venetian Republic compares with any Royal portrait elsewhere for its sense of dignity and authority.

The painting of this picture is extraordinary, with its strongly marked feeling of vitality combined with a very beautiful colour scheme. Another characteristic of Bellini worthy of note is that he was one of the first artists to introduce landscapes in his religious pictures. An interesting example of this may be seen in the National Gallery in his " Christ's Agony in the Garden."

On November 29, 1516, Giovanni Bellini died not far short of ninety.

IOANNES BELLINVS

Sandro Botticelli
1444-1510

THIS great artist, whose family name was dei Filippi, and signed his pictures " Sandro di Marino," is known everywhere by his nickname, Botticelli—the little barrel—from the shop sign over the door of his father's tannery in Florence. Botticelli, one of the most fascinating figures in the history of Art, was born in Florence in 1444, the Florence of Lorenzo the Magnificent, one of the greatest patrons of the Arts. After a short apprenticeship to his brother Antonio, a goldsmith, the young Sandro became the favourite pupil of the celebrated Fra Filippo Lippi, the painter monk, then working at Prato. Botticelli became famous in his time, and among his important commissions was the decoration of the Sistine Chapel, in Rome, where he resided for a few years, being paid large sums which, however, he appears to have squandered.

The middle of the fifteenth century was a period of great changes, and the starting of even greater developments. The Turks had just seized Constantinople, an event which had no small reaction in Florence, already in the throes of civil and religious strife. Botticelli was one of those who, in these differences, became a partizan of Fra Savonarola, the revolutionary Dominican preacher, but the death of the latter, at the stake, was a blow from which the great painter never recovered. He lived on for another ten years, often in great poverty, from which he was relieved, at times, by his great patron, Lorenzo de Medici.

There are hardly fifty works definitely attributable to him, and of these his " Madonna of the Magnificat," in the Uffizi Gallery, Florence, is perhaps his most popular religious masterpiece, and " The Birth of Venus," here illustrated, is undoubtedly the most celebrated of his non-religious pictures. The Florentines were especially interested in the revival of Greek learning, and Botticelli was one of the painters who were fond of re-creating the stories of the ancient gods—hence the rendering of " The Birth of Venus." It must not be taken for a realistic picture of an actual occurrence, but only for a fanciful and poetic version of an old world legend, treated conventionally.

MADAME DE POMPADOUR

By FRANÇOIS BOUCHER

In the National Gallery of Scotland, Edinburgh—French School

François Boucher
1703-1770

THE art of the eighteenth century in France owed its inspiration and patronage almost entirely to the gay and pleasure-seeking court of Louis XV, at Versailles, and, to a great extent, to the influence of Madame de Pompadour. One is not, therefore, surprised to find that the general tendency of painting in France, at that time, followed the lead of its patrons, and the last thing one would expect was any form of religious art.

The coterie of literary men at the Court, encouraged by the Pompadour, gave rise to a vogue for an artificial love of the countryside, and it was in this atmosphere that the work of Boucher, and others, was produced.

François Boucher, large hearted and pleasure loving, who stands as one of the great decorative artists nicknamed " The Glory of Paris," was born in that city on September 29, 1703, and seems to have been well suited to the times in which he lived. His father, Nicolas Boucher, a somewhat ordinary painter, none too prosperous, sent his son, at seventeen, to the studio of Lemoyne, who painted some of the ceilings at Versailles. From this master, whom Boucher loved and admired to the end of his days, he acquired his broad decorative style of painting and became so skilled, in a very short time, that it was difficult to distinguish his works from those of his master. In his nineteenth year, Boucher left Lemoyne's studio an accomplished artist and, having secured the first prize at the French Academy, he went to Rome in the company of Carl Van Loo. Like other French painters, Boucher does not seem to have been greatly impressed or influenced by the Italian masters, and he had the courage to declare on his return, four years later, that he " had found Michael-Angelo contorted, Raphael insipid, and Correggio gloomy," a rather amusing verdict, in one so young. So back again in Paris, bringing with him a large collection of religious pictures which were hailed by the critics and the Academy for their beauty and virility, Boucher soon saw that in the atmosphere of gaiety and frivolity of the Court and of his beloved Paris, the public had little taste for historical and religious pictures. He immediately turned his attention to the painting of mytholog-

(*Continued*)

PORTRAIT OF A YOUNG WOMAN

By FRANÇOIS BOUCHER

In the Louvre—French School

ical subjects treated in a rather frivolous manner, which was what his patrons at Court desired. It is true that there was another camp at Court which, more inclined to serious pursuits, severely criticised Boucher for the subject matter of his pictures as being too licentious : for all that, he was a gifted artist, did not profess to be a moralist, and was certainly not a hypocrite.

Boucher was thoroughly in love with his art, and was a prodigious worker, often remaining at his easel twelve hours at a time : he used to say " My Studio is my Church." He was one of the rare examples of a man whose recreation was his work, he played as he worked, and out of this untiring industry he made ample for his pleasures, but his kind, generous nature prevented him becoming a rich man. At the age of thirty, Boucher married a woman called Marie Jeanne Buseau, a pretty Parisienne who often sat for him as the shapely figure of Psyche, and had some fame as a miniaturist.

When 40, Boucher was not only at the zenith of his powers, but also of his fortune. As he was a favourite of the Pompadour, of whom he made many portraits, commissions of all kinds were showered upon him and the next ten years were for him a triumphal procession during which he created masterpieces which certainly place him in the front rank of the painters of his age as a decorative painter.

The exquisite portrait of La Pompadour, here shown, which the National Gallery of Scotland so fortunately possesses, is surely a triumph of graceful design and brilliant colour, and one can well imagine that even this much-flattered lady must have been enormously pleased with the result.

Our second colour plate, " Portrait of a Young Woman," in the Louvre, Paris, is said by some authorities to be also a portrait of Madame de Pom-padour, probably a later study than the Edinburgh picture. It contains in her features perhaps a hint of those anxieties about her precarious position which she was at such pains to conceal.

By the year 1768, the painter's health was failing him ; a ghost of his former jovial self, his sight going, he suffered many ills. He was dis-covered, dead, on a morning in May, 1770, in his sixty-sixth year, seated at his easel before a sketch of Venus, with the brush fallen from his hand. Diderot, his life-long arch enemy wrote : " I have spoken too much ill of Boucher, I retract."

Ford Madox Brown
1821-1893

WHEN Ford Madox Brown was a youth, figure painting in this country was at a low ebb, and it was fortunate for him that he was born in Calais and educated in Belgium, where his powerful sense of decorative drawing and colour was not frustrated by narrow conventions. As a young man, he returned to England ready to undertake great works, but his suggested cartoons for Westminster Hall were not accepted.

In a mood of disappointment, he went to Italy, and further consolidated his powers there; and on his way home, in 1845, his wife died in Paris.

He had a profound influence on Rossetti, and although he was not a member of the Pre-Raphaelite Brethren it is said that they looked to him as a master, and that the very word Pre-Raphaelite was first used by him. This movement was an attempt to return to the methods of early Italian masters prior to Raphael, and was of very short duration.

" The Last of England " is a picture in which there is a strong blend of feeling and technique. The picture owes its origin to the great emigration movement which reached its height in 1852. Brown travelled to Gravesend to say farewell to his great friend, Thomas Woolner, who later became famous as sculptor and poet. Although this is a small picture for Brown, it is full of detail, all of which is exquisitely painted, the clothes of the two emigrants being most realistically rendered, the title of the picture being all too clearly readable in the two sad faces. Among other important pictures by this artist is "Work," a sort of pictorial chant to the dignity of labour; "Romeo and Juliet," "The Entombment," "Chaucer Reciting His Poetry," "The Execution of Mary Queen of Scots," and in 1852, the fine "Christ Washing St. Peter's Feet."

Towards the end of his life, Brown was commissioned to paint the history of Manchester in a series of twelve frescoes for the Town Hall. He is prominent among those artists with a fine sense of the drama of life, and his art in consequence is infused with a certain feeling of movement. He was also a good linguist and poet. He died on October 6, 1893, a disappointed man.

Sir Edward Coley Burne-Jones, R.A.
1833-1898

THE work of Sir Edward Burne-Jones places this artist somewhat apart from the main current of English nineteenth-century painting. His was a romantic and religious temperament. Intended for the church, a chance acquaintanceship with Rossetti changed his life. Coming under this artist's influence, after leaving Oxford, Burne-Jones began to paint seriously, seeking inspiration in old poems, ballads, and sacred legends. So assiduously did he work that he soon won for himself a high place among contemporary artists, and a tour in Italy, where he found some spiritual kinship with the Siennese and Florentine schools, helped him to form his style and enlarge his vision.

" King Cophetua " is one of his most important and best paintings. It is instinct with reverence for the beauty of human love. Planned and designed to accentuate the romantic story of the powerful king who surrenders his heart to the obscure girl, we see the king, in all his power, sitting at the feet of the maiden of his choice. He holds his crown humbly in his hands. To the right of the picture are his lance and shield. The beggar-maid, clad in her poor garments, takes her place above him. She is pensive and full of wonder at a dream that has become a reality. Mute witnesses of this strange scene, two figures on a balcony look down, and would appear to be giving it their benediction. Through an open doorway, in the top right-hand corner of the picture, a delicately painted landscape can be observed.

This work, which was completed in 1884, was presented to the Tate Gallery by a group of admirers after the artist's death. Although Burne-Jones lived a somewhat retired life, he found several discerning patrons. Many of his pictures commanded unusually high prices. " The Beguiling of Merlin," for instance, was sold during the artist's lifetime for £3,750.

Although Burne-Jones painted large pictures, he still retained an enthusiasm for infinite detail, such as may be seen in " The Star of Bethlehem." His mind had some kinship with the monastic illuminator, and his methods of working without considering the expense of time was also characteristic of

(Continued)

THE STAR OF BETHLEHEM

By SIR EDWARD COLEY BURNE-JONES, R.A.

In the Museum and Art Gallery, Birmingham—British School

By kind permission of the Birmingham Corporation Art Gallery Committee

the middle ages. In " The Star of Bethlehem " we can see with what consideration he studied every minute fragment from the thatch on the roof of the hut to the robes and gifts of the Wise Men. There is a veritable garden of flowers in this picture, the rendering of which is both precise and poetic. It was such a subject that he loved to linger over like a craftsman who would not hasten the completion of his task because of the joy it gave him.

Some of Burne-Jones' pictures remained with him for years. " The Prioress' Tale," for instance, was begun in 1869 and was not finished until 1898. This artist's method of work was the same as that followed by some of the old Italian masters. He drew first in chalk or pencil, making many figure studies, details of drapery, costume, furniture, and flowers.

He delighted in jewels and the rich chasing of armour and weapons. He would learn all these things by heart, as it were, while their composition and arrangement were dawning in his mind. He would then prepare a water-colour, the same size as the intended oil-painting. Using this as a guide, Burne-Jones went about his final task, building up his picture like a mosaic. The devotion or sincerity on the part of this artist communicates itself to the spectator, and compels his admiration.

Burne-Jones was never a facile painter in the sense that he could handle paint with the fluent ease of a Rubens or a Sargent. He started his studentship too late for that and, save for the help of Rossetti, he was self-taught. He evolved his own technique, but it suited perfectly his leisurely, beautiful, and somewhat melancholy mind.

Burne-Jones' paintings are only a part of this artist's prodigious output. He did much decorative work in collaboration with William Morris, designing stained-glass windows for churches in Sloane Street and Vere Street, London. There is stained-glass of his in Oxford and Salisbury Cathedrals and some in the Cambridge colleges. The American Protestant Church in Rome contains his most ambitious effort in ecclesiastical decoration, viz., the fine series of mosaics which adorn the apse and the walls. Burne-Jones had a great influence on some of his contemporaries, and although it began to wane, his centenary exhibition, held last year, revived an interest in his peculiar gifts and reaffirmed his title to greatness.

Lady Elizabeth Butler

1845-1933

THE reputation Lady Butler (Miss Elizabeth Thompson) achieved with her two famous pictures, "The Roll Call" and "Scotland for Ever," was immediate and astonishing. Her triumphs challenge anything attempted in fiction. The stories told in her "Autobiography" are, to us, almost unbelievable. All society fêted her. From Queen Victoria and the Royal Family downward, through all classes honours and praises were showered upon her. In those days there were no warring factions, no dissentients. Crowds lingered all day, spellbound, before her pictures at the Royal Academy, whilst others strove to get a glimpse of them. Officers vied in lending their chargers to paint from, and sitters competed for the honour of being represented in one of her canvases. It was a time of military enthusiasms and of great pride in our martial achievements. We were constantly engaged in petty warfare in some part of the far-off world. The volunteer movement had become the fashionable "rage." Society itself was a military stronghold.

Lady Butler's husband, as all the world knows, was a distinguished and active general. Fighting was going on in Zululand at the moment Lady Butler conceived her idea for the famous Waterloo charge of the Scots Greys. She tells us she owed the subject to an impulse she received when at the private view at the Grosvenor Galleries. In her own words, " I felt myself getting more and more annoyed while perambulating those rooms, and to such a point of exasperation was I impelled, that I fairly fled and, breathing the honest air of Bond Street, took a hansom to my studio. There I pinned a seven-foot sheet of brown paper on an old canvas and, with a piece of charcoal and a piece of white chalk, flung the charge of The Greys upon it."

The picture was just begun when Lady Butler received a commission from Queen Victoria to paint her almost equally popular " Rorke's Drift." When the latter was completed, Lady Butler took up " Scotland for Ever " again, and finished it. It was painted whilst in residence at Plymouth Hoe, where her husband, General Sir William Butler, was adjutant-general.

Jean Baptiste Siméon Chardin
1699-1779

UNLIKE most of the painters of this period, Chardin was nothing of a Court favourite, indeed he was all his life a plain artist, of the people. He was born on November 2, 1699, the son of Jean Chardin, a very skilful carpenter who intended all his sons to follow his calling; but, to his consternation, the second son, Siméon, showed decided tendencies towards painting, and, after the usual struggle in such cases, the boy was sent to the studio of Cazes, a rather mediocre artist.

The life of Chardin was consistent throughout : he was of a kindly, honest and generous nature, and his work is stamped with sincerity.

He was a master of still-life subjects in which he painted simple objects with a consummate skill and dignity and a special point of interest in these homely studies is that, when he painted a loaf of bread, and other simple things on a cottage table, there was always a subtle suggestion of human presence in the room. His first exhibited pictures of this kind were a great success, the critics recording that " a new master has arisen rivalling the Dutch painters." Encouraged by friends, Chardin sought election to the Academy, and, on submitting his pictures to its members, was unanimously elected, the entrance fees even being reduced owing to his lack of means. The same lack of means delayed his marriage with Marguerite Saintar, which took place in 1731 : but she only lived four years. Chardin was a short, muscular man with a round jovial face, very reserved, but implicitly trusted by all who came in contact with him; his generosity was proverbial, he was incapable of any sort of avarice or greed. Such a man not only could never grow rich, but was inevitably destined for hard times which arrived in 1741, when he became very ill. The loss of his wife and little girl was a great blow to him and, his mother dying shortly after, he was alone until 1744, when he married a widow, Françoise Pouget, a very business-like person who put his home in order; but, although he owned his house, his affairs went from bad to worse, as his pension was not regularly paid. Chardin died on December 6, 1779. He was buried at St. Germain l'Auxerrois.

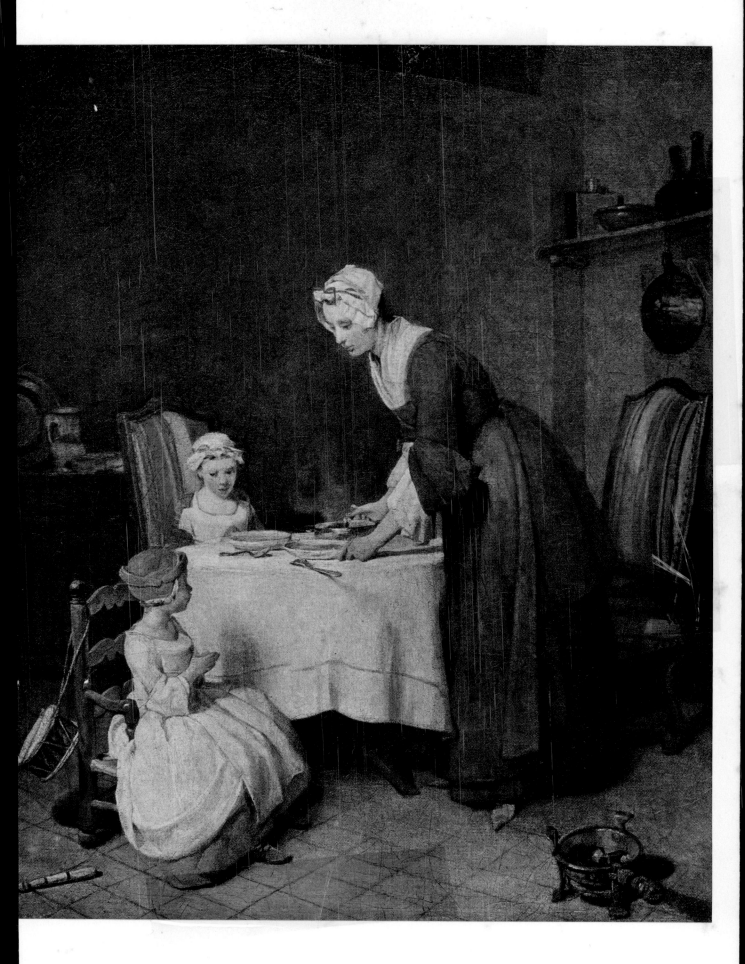

John Constable, R.A.
1776-1831

WHEN John Constable was born, landscape painting, save for the work of Richard Wilson and Gainsborough, was uninspired. It had become formalised and dead. Constable revived it, and he was not only one of our greatest landscape painters, but the pioneer of a vital style that founded a whole school of modern painting. It is no exaggeration to say that the French Impressionists first saw the "light" in the work of this famous Englishman.

When the " Hay Wain " was exhibited in Paris in 1821, it was highly praised and influenced the course of French painting for nearly a century. It is a sad commentary on English critical taste that Constable first found honour outside his own country. He put his brush on the very pulse of nature, escaping many pitfalls and defying tradition.

He was born at East Bergholt in 1776. Much of his work comes fresh from the beautiful scenery of this corner of Suffolk, and some of his subjects can be identified even to-day.

The son of a miller, he worked at first for his father, but his genius for painting being irrespressible, he came to London to consolidate the technique he had acquired in his leisure moments. The originality of his outlook and his powerful method of handling paint, retarded his recognition as an artist, and he sold few of his pictures.

In 1816, he married Mary Bicknell, who eventually inherited £20,000 from her father which enabled Constable to devote himself without fret and hindrance to his ideals.

He was a great worker, making innumerable small sketches in pencil, water-colours and oils of every aspect of nature. From these he built up a series of large pictures of incomparable loveliness. What he could not sell during his lifetime is now worth many thousands of pounds.

One secret of Constable's power as a painter is that he had time and inclination to look closely at nature before he began to study the old Masters. Somewhere he writes : " I constantly observe that a man who will not

(*Continued*)

submit to a long toil in the imitation of nature flies off, becomes a phantom, and produces dreams of nonsense and abortions."

Again, on April 8, 1826, Constable writes to his friend and patron, John Fisher : " I have dispatched a large landscape to the Academy, upright, of the size of ' The Lock,' but a subject of very different nature : inland cornfields, a close lane forming the foreground ; it is not neglected in any part : the trees are more than usually studied, well defined, as well as the stems; they are shaken by a pleasant and healthful breeze at noon."

This picture, " The Cornfield," was presented to the Nation by friends of Constable after the artist's death. It is perhaps the best known of all his work, and expresses a homely scene in robust pictorial language. The trees throughout are painted with intense care and realistic effect. The little shepherd-boy, who has left his flock a moment while he drinks at a spring, and the workers in the cornfield, are part of the changeless activity of rustic life. In the distance a square-towered church and some cottages complete the view. It is a scene such as exists to this day round about East Bergholt.

In spite of modern traffic, the ubiquity of the machine, it is possible in Suffolk to recapture the sentiments that Constable expressed. He was endowed with the heart of a poet and the eye of a naturalist, and there was no detail of tree, weed, flower, sky, or water that escaped his creative imagination. He was elected an A.R.A. in 1819 and R.A. ten years later. He died at the age of 61 and is buried at Hampstead, where he lived for some years.

There are two houses in London still standing where Constable lived, one at Well Walk, Hampstead, his " dear Hampstead," his " sweet Hampstead," as he called it. On this modest dwelling he writes : " My little studio commands a view without equal in Europe." It is certainly a magnificent prospect, either towards London or the north, and, even to-day, we can still imagine how the painter must have enjoyed the panorama from the top windows. Hampstead in Constable's time was a rural village, although there was a fairly frequent 'bus or coach to town.

The other house is in Charlotte Street, Fitzroy Square, a neighbourhood much affected by artists at the beginning of last century. The pilgrim in search of Constable will find a commemoration plaque on both these houses.

SOUVENIR D'ITALIE

By JEAN BAPTISTE CAMILLE COROT

In the Louvre—French School

Jean Baptiste Camille Corot
1796-1875

COROT, the great French romantic landscape painter, was born on July 20, 1796, the son of a wigmaker, rather a commonplace man, who was all his life puzzled at the ambition of his son to become a painter and, later on, no less puzzled at his success. However, having become reconciled to the inevitable, he had the good sense to make a small allowance to his son from his savings, for the " degrading business," as he called it. The young man, being of a contented and happy disposition, had no difficulty in making this allowance satisfy his simple needs; in any case, whatever he had then, or later, was always at the disposal of any friend with a greater need. Indeed, the stories of his endless generosities, and especially to those who might be counted as possible rivals, are too numerous to mention.

Following the example of artists of many lands, he was drawn to Italy on more than one occasion, but was not to be unduly influenced by the masters whose works he studied there, and all his life he remained an individual type.

The type in question was that of a supremely poetical and romantic painter. His art presents a marked contrast to that of our English Turner, who gloried in attempts to paint the sun and its effects on Nature; on the contrary, Corot had almost a physical fear of actual sunlight, except in its more subtle and subdued aspects. He was a painter of quiet tones and colours rather than brilliant colourful schemes.

Our colour plate, " Souvenir d'Italie," has, in its very title, a hint of the artist's love for Italy, but the picture itself, in its general treatment, is more French than Italian and is a typical example of the romantic landscapes which Corot loved to paint.

Like many other great painters, Corot developed his genius more and more as he grew older, and to the end of his life he remained of a beautiful and childlike disposition which endeared him to all who came in contact with him; he was evidently so conscious that, as he aged, his powers increased that he actually looked forward to a future life in which he hoped that " at any rate, we shall go on painting up there." He died in his eightieth year.

THE MYSTIC MARRIAGE OF ST. CATHERINE

By ANTONIO DA CORREGGIO

In the Louvre—School of Parma

/

Antonio da Correggio
1494-1534

ANTONIO ALLEGRI DA CORREGGIO was named after his birthplace, il Correggio, a small town in Northern Italy. He was the son of a cloth merchant and is said to have been a pupil of Francesco Bianchi, of Modena.

It can hardly be said that his examples of religious art are marked by a spirit of devotion, though they are notable for charm of composition, with a sense of movement, a rare beauty of colour and graceful types of figures.

" The Mystic Marriage of St. Catherine," in the Louvre, Paris, reproduced here, illustrates the legend.

The Infant Christ, who is seen placing the wedding ring on the finger of the kneeling St. Catherine, on the right, in a golden robe. The figure behind her is that of St. Sebastian, holding in his hands arrows, symbols of his martyrdom.

This picture was at one time in the royal collection brought together by Charles I, at Hampton Court Palace, which, after the execution of the king, was for the most part allowed to be dispersed.

Correggio was an undoubted genius and occupies a somewhat isolated position among all the artists in Italy. He was strangely independent and original, for his chief interest was the study of beauty in feminine form, which was so marked a feature of eighteenth-century art in France.

Little is known of his youth, but at the early age of 20 he was already painting important commissions.

He married in 1520, Girolama Merlini, a girl of his native town, daughter of an equerry to the Duke of Mantua, and had a son. He died in 1534, in his fortieth year, having at that early age placed to his credit a remarkable achievement in great works, which are to be found in most of the European galleries, such as " Danaë," in Rome; " Night," in Dresden; and " Mercury instructing Cupid in the presence of Venus," in the London National Gallery.

Frederic Cotman
1850-1920

THE name of Cotman stands very high in the history of British art, foremost among them, of course, is John Sell Cotman, a master in water-colours and oil paint. His two sons, Miles Edmund and Joseph John, followed in their father's footsteps. But Frederic Cotman, John Sell's nephew, had a different style. Whereas the others were best at landscape work, he was more interested in the figure and subject pictures.

His picture, " One of the Family," is a popular example of his realistic manner and shows accomplishment in grouping and lighting. The human interest, the carefully observed poses and character, the contrast of youth and age, the details of the table, shimmering in light from the door and window, the well-drawn horse and dog, are evidence of a quite remarkable skill.

This well-known picture is a good example of what is generally called a picture which tells a story. As this style was particularly acceptable fifty years ago it is often described as " Victorian"; indeed, every one will have noticed that this kind of pictorial narrative is now rather rare.

Frederic Cotman was born in 1850. Like his uncle and cousins he showed early a talent for drawing, and worked at Ipswich. When he was eighteen, he became a student at the Royal Academy Schools, winning a gold medal there in 1873. He exhibited at the Royal Academy from 1871 to 1904, and at the Liverpool Autumn Exhibition intermittently between 1873 and 1909. He also won a silver medal at l'Exposition Universelle, Paris, in 1889, and was a member of the Royal Institute, London.

" One of the Family " was first shown at the Royal Academy in 1880, and appeared later in the year at the Liverpool Autumn Exhibition; it was subsequently purchased for the famous Walker Art Gallery in that city.

Frederic George Cotman worked chiefly at St. Ives (Huntingdonshire) and in London, and died in nineteen-twenty, at the age of seventy years.

David Cox
1783-1859

BRITISH artists, by common consent, have been pre-eminent in the practice of the very difficult art of water-colour painting, and the two following plates are examples of one of the most gifted of our water-colourists.

David Cox, born on April 29, 1783, was of humble origin, his father being a blacksmith; at an early age the lad went to his father's forge, but was unable to continue there as, owing to his delicate health, the work was too hard. Having broken a leg, he employed his convalescence experimenting with a paint-box, which had been given him, and that decided him to become a painter.

At the age of 15, he was apprenticed to a manufacturer of fancy goods, where he showed much skill in decorative work; but the suicide of his master terminated his apprenticeship and threw him on his own resources.

His next employment was as a scene-painter's labourer, at Birmingham, in the theatre of the elder Macready. A little later when, special scenery being required, the scene-painter De Maria of the Italian Opera House, London, was called to Birmingham, he was so struck by young Cox's ability that he allowed the lad to assist him, and it was not long before the young artist was promoted scene-painter to the theatre.

After working four years in this manner, Cox went to London and there met John Varlet, another water-colour artist, from whom he learnt much of his art, and in 1805 he was painting landscapes in North Wales, in which district he painted many of his best works. An exhibition of these paintings at an art dealer's in London brought him a patron in Colonel Windsor, afterwards the Earl of Plymouth, and from that time he gave up his work as a scene-painter.

In 1808 David Cox married his landlady's daughter, Mary Ragg, and, taking a cottage at Dulwich, he started producing quantities of drawings which he sold to teachers for use in schools; it was only by great effort in the production and sale of these sketches that he was able to make a bare living.

(Continued)

In the year 1813, Cox was elected to the Old Water-colour Society, and shortly afterwards he applied for the post of drawing master of the Military College at Farnham. This appointment, however, did not last very long, as it necessitated being away from home; and, on returning to London and finding that all his pupils had disappeared, he was driven to seek a post of drawing master at a girl's school in Hereford, at a salary of £100 a year. There, by the aid of a little borrowed money, he settled in a small cottage where, although in great poverty, he worked for thirteen years.

Returning eventually to London, he settled in Kennington, where he not only found pupils, but sold his work freely. When near sixty years of age, he determined to make a plunge in the direction he had always desired and, leaving London in 1841, he settled in the neighbourhood of Birmingham, and, while his son retained the pupils in London, he devoted himself in great happiness entirely to his painting. It was during this period that he painted his best-known masterpieces and year after year he went to Bettws-y-Coed, of which there are so many happy recollections.

It was during this period—in 1842—that he painted " Harlech Castle," the subject of one of our reproductions, a very lovely study in which the characteristics of Welsh coast scenery are at once noticeable. There is a sense of movement and vitality in the trees and shrubs, here, which one is never conscious of even in the finest photograph from nature. By the courtesy of the Keeper of the Birmingham Museum and Art Gallery, we are permitted to reproduce, as a companion subject, " The Skirt of the Forest," which was painted by David Cox thirteen years later, for it will be seen that it is signed and dated 1855, but four years before the artist's death, when he was 72 years of age. This beautiful and tenderly rendered picture far from showing any decline in the artist's powers, seems, on the contrary, to indicate a development of his artistic vision and breadth of treatment.

The year 1845 brought him the great sorrow of the loss of his wife at the age of 74, and another blow followed when he was seized with apoplexy which left his sight and memory much impaired.

It was in June, 1859, that he took to his bed and his last words were " Good-bye, pictures," after which he passed away peacefully in his sleep.

Leonardo da Vinci
1452-1519

WE come now to the greatest name in Art, with the exception of Michael-Angelo, both of them so well known : Leonardo rather by his works than his name, Michael-Angelo by his name rather than his works.

Leonardo is considered to have been the greatest intellectual genius in history, certainly a brief account of his achievements in science and art would fill many pages of this book. By reason of the many subjects of which he was a master, the total number of his genuine paintings is small.

Leonardo was born—1452—in the village of Vinci, from which he derives his name, for he was the illegitimate son of a notary, Ser Piero, of the same place. About the year 1470, the young artist entered the studio of the great painter and sculptor, Verrocchio, but it was not long before he rivalled his master completely. It is related that Verrocchio, when painting his celebrated " Baptism of Christ " allowed his pupil to paint one of the angels and, being so amazed at the result, declared that he himself " would never again take pencil in his hand."

It will be generally agreed that the two most famous pictures in the world are Leonardo's " Last Supper " and " Mona Lisa." The name Leonardo da Vinci instantly brings to mind these two works and, even to those who would not know the artist's name, the pictures are old favourites; it seems fitting, therefore, that these two masterpieces should appear in this volume.

Possibly the most beloved picture in the world is " The Last Supper," painted in the refectory of the Dominican Convent of St. Maria delle Grazie, in Milan. Finished in 1498, it is sad to record that this lovely mural painting, with its great appeal to all who see it, showed signs of decay within fifty years of its completion, and that it has suffered not a little since at the hands of " restorers." Even to-day, as our plate shows, it is far more than a noble ruin.

It will be noticed that this composition was, to put it mildly, not improved by the cutting of a doorway in the centre lower portion, and in later years the cavalry of the Emperor Napoleon still further added to the damage to this work, when they were stabled in the refectory of the monastery, although it is recorded that Napoleon gave definite orders that the picture should be respected. This picture has been the model for innumerable versions of the subject, very few of which have approached it in quality.

The famous "Mona Lisa," our frontispiece, the greatest treasure in the Louvre, was the portrait of the third wife of Francesco Del Giocondo, and is sometimes called "La Joconde." It is said that the artist "loitered over the picture for four years," and that he insisted on having entertainers near the lady to sing and play, or otherwise amuse her; the result certainly appears to be that she seems intensely interested, though whether she be actually smiling or not, has always been a matter of discussion and much controversy.

The picture was bought by Francis I of France, and, it may be remembered, was stolen from the Louvre in 1912, but was later mysteriously restored to the Gallery.

Another masterpiece in the Louvre is Leonardo's "The Virgin of the Rocks," painted in 1482, in his thirtieth year. It was executed to the order of the Brotherhood of the Conception at Saint Francesco, in Milan, and appears to have been a subject of dispute between the artist and the Brotherhood as to the price to be paid for it, with the result that the picture was withdrawn and sold to the King of France for the price demanded, and this accounts for its presence in the Louvre.

In order to satisfy the Brotherhood in Milan, a second version of the same picture was painted, at the price they were willing to pay, and this version, which in 1777 was brought to England by Gavin Hamilton, who sold it to the Marquess of Lansdowne, is the well-known picture now in the National Gallery, which acquired it in 1880 for the small sum of nine thousand pounds. It has been already remarked that owing to the prodigious activities of Da Vinci in every imaginable art and science, the list of his admitted pictures is a short one, therefore it is by great fortune that the Diploma Gallery, in Burlington House, should possess one of his most supremely beautiful drawings which is the sketch for "The Virgin and Child with St.

Anne and St. John," which is worth a visit to the Gallery for its own sake alone.

The universal genius of Leonardo is almost beyond belief; every subject he took up he excelled in, apparently without effort, and there is scarcely any branch of human activity in which he took no interest. In addition to his skill as painter and sculptor, he was a brilliant musician, and well versed in mathematics, architecture, and, at one time, was busy evolving a flying machine. He was not only a prolific writer, but was engaged from time to time by his Royal Patrons in the construction of fortified positions.

Leonardo da Vinci was a man of splendid physique and great personal beauty, with the engaging manners of a diplomat. His physical strength indeed was so wonderful that he could break a horseshoe with his fingers, and yet his touch was so gentle and sensitive that he could perform brilliantly on many musical instruments. An odd peculiarity about this unique man was that he not only was left-handed, but wrote from right to left. Although he was one who scorned the mere pursuit of money, he had a just estimate of his own marvellous powers, and it is of interest to read the account of his offer of service to Ludovici Sforza, Duke of Milan, in which he sets out his qualifications which included : " Scientist, architect, painter, sculptor, and military engineer," to which he might have added many another; and it is significant to note that in this he puts scientist first, whereas we to-day know him chiefly as one of the greatest painters and sculptors ever known. This busy man also could find time to design and direct the great pageants which were a recurrent feature of the life of his day.

In 1516, Francis I persuaded Leonardo to return to France with him as his court painter. He never returned to his native land, nor was his stay in France a long one, as he died three years later, it is said, in the King's arms.

MADONNA OF THE HARPIES

By ANDREA DEL SARTO

In the Uffizi Gallery—School of Florence

Andrea del Sarto
1486-1531

THIS artist was blessed with many names, but is usually called Andrea d'Agnolo, or Andrea del Sarto. He was born in Florence in 1486. He was the son of a tailor, this accounts for his nickname, Sarto, which in Italian means tailor. At an early age, he was sent to a goldsmith to learn the art of engraving on metal; later, he came under the serious training of Piero di Cosimo, from whom he learnt to paint, especially the lovely landscapes which are a feature in many of his pictures. One of Del Sarto's first great achievements was a series of frescoes, or wall paintings, illustrating the life of St. John the Baptist and, owing to the technical perfection of his drawing and painting, he came to be known as "Andrea the perfect painter," a title not undeserved in many ways for he was a very great artist until he became tempted to follow too closely the great Michael Angelo.

About 1516, Del Sarto painted a picture of the Dead Christ, which was so much admired by Francis I of France that he induced the artist to go to Paris, where he was greatly honoured and royally entertained by the king. But he had already married, before leaving Florence, a worthless and extravagant woman, named Lucretia del Fede, who was to be the cause of his downfall. In 1519, she begged him to obtain leave of absence from the French court, which was granted. On his return home, he soon forgot his obligations to the King of France and embarked on a series of wild extravagances with his wife and friends, and it was not long before he had squandered all he had. Stung by remorse and the desertion of his so-called friends, and later of his wife, he became a prey to despondency. His life was ended by an attack of plague in 1531, when he was but 44 years of age. His masterpiece, the beautiful group entitled " The Madonna of the Harpies," here illustrated, is a majestic composition. It derives its name from the four harpies which appear on the sculptured pedestal on which the Madonna stands.

It is said that her face is an idealised portrait of the artist's wife, and it is thought that the face of St. John the Evangelist, on the right, is the artist himself; and the figure on the left, holding a cross, represents St. Francis.

HARMONY

By SIR FRANK DICKSEE, P.R.A.

In the Tate Gallery—British School

Sir Frank Dicksee, P.R.A.
1853-1928

THE poetic meaning of this picture is apparent, alike in its title and subject, and it could be taken for an illustration to the opening line of *Twelfth Night*, " If music be the food of love, play on." The artist has brought together all the essentials of romance—the young lovers in medieval costumes, the musical instrument, and the stained-glass window in which is dimly perceived a design of the Madonna and Child. The light filtering through the stained glass tinges the whole scene with a certain mystical atmosphere. The girl's head is skilfully framed by the window, her auburn hair and pensive profile contrasting with the dark hair and rapt expression of her admirer.

Although much of the picture is in shadow, there is a great wealth of subdued colour from dark green to luminous crimson, from yellow to blue. The action of the girl's arms is particularly realistic, and the artist has made the most of the light from the window to aid him in revealing the form of the hands and forearms.

This picture, which was painted by Frank Dicksee when he was a young man, brought the artist a great popular success, which he consolidated during the course of a long life with various other subject pictures and portraits of beautiful women.

The wide popularity of " Harmony " is not difficult to understand, for romantic love tales are still sought for by the great public, and as artists are no longer inclined to paint them, men and women find what they seek in the "pictures " of the cinema.

" Harmony " was the happy composition upon which Sir Frank Dicksee founded his artistic fortune, and he achieved the cherished desire of all artists—the presidency of the Royal Academy—in 1924, and received the honour of knighthood a year later. Being a man of distinguished appearance and manner, he was an ideal president. He passed away on October 3, 1928, the last representative of an epoch, for with him the school of well-known Victorian narrative painters practically came to an end.

THE ADORATION OF THE MAGI

By ALBRECHT DÜRER

In the Uffizi Gallery—German School

Albrecht Dürer
1471-1528

IN the lovely old city of Nuremberg, on May 21, 1471, there was born Albrecht Dürer, whose father was a goldsmith of that town.

At an early age, Albrecht Dürer, after a short period in his father's workshop, was apprenticed in the studio of Michael Wolgemut, where he was far from happy; and, on leaving, he devoted himself to painting and especially to portrait painting. His masterpiece, painted in 1504, "The Adoration of the Magi," here reproduced, is probably his most beautiful composition, influenced, no doubt, by a memorable visit which he paid to Venice.

In 1493, when twenty-three years of age, Dürer married Agnes Frey, a clever, practical woman, but never at anytime, had a family of his own, which was perhaps fortunate for him, in a way, as, at the age of 31, on the death of his father, his mother and a host of younger brothers and sisters were thrown upon his care. It was probably owing to this new responsibility that Dürer decided, as many a man has done before and since, that painting would not be sufficient to meet his needs, and he turned his attention to wood-engraving, in which art his genius came to full maturity, for he was a master of line.

His good wife was of great assistance to him in the sale of these wood-cuts, which, even in his lifetime, had an enormous vogue. What the poor struggling artist would have thought, or said, of the huge prices paid at auction sales to-day for these woodcuts, one can but guess!

His active mind led him to a scientific quest for beauty, but after a while he gave up the search. "Beauty! What is it, I know not," he said. Studying Nature direct, as every artist should, he came to the conclusion that "Art lies hid in Nature, he who can pluck it makes it his."

An extremely handsome man of good build and somewhat of a dandy in his day, Dürer was also of untiring industry, honourable, unselfish, of a sweet disposition, and deeply religious; he was probably not unaware of his good appearance, for he was very fond of producing self-portraits, some of which —especially one in Munich and another in Madrid—are famous. He died suddenly in 1528, on April 6, in his native city, mourned by all who knew him.

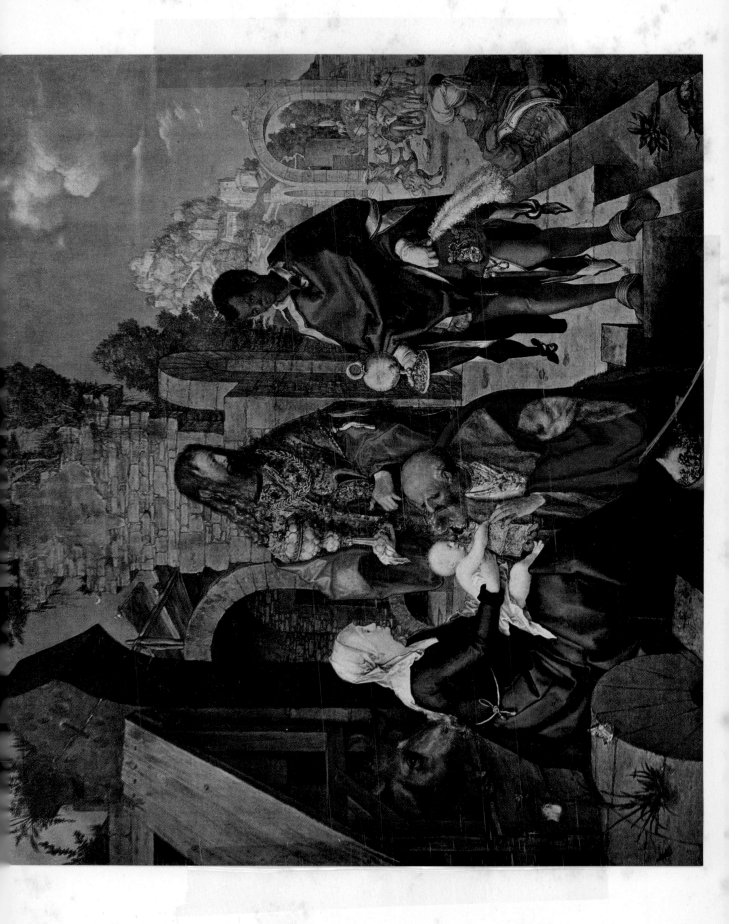

POPLARS IN A THAMES VALLEY

By SIR ALFRED EAST, A.R.A.

In the Aberdeen Art Gallery—British School

Sir Alfred East, A.R.A.

1849-1913

ALONG the reaches of the Upper Thames are thousands of pretty scenes, such as the subject of Sir Alfred East's " Poplars in a Thames Valley." In journeying upstream the river unfolds before us like a silken ribbon, flowing now through level meads, now past fields bordered with low hills, past islets whose overhanging branches shelter the peaceful backwaters sought by lovers, the haunt of the kingfisher and the coot, where many a match has been arranged, helped by the heart-moving beauty of the scene.

Poplars are a feature of many of the river's prettiest reaches, and they have never failed to allure painters of Thames scenery. At eventide their tall forms catch the light or sway in the breeze, and are generally found sentinelling some old country house or farmstead. Sometimes they stand dark against the sky, as in our picture, where we see their reflections broken by the currents in the water. We note how observantly the painter has rendered these currents, picking up the heavy rain-charged clouds that are streaming over the little township with its spired church and bridge. Whenever rain is about, it is seldom far off in the valley of the Thames. The river's course inevitably attracts clouds, and at evening their beauty enhances the splendour of the pageant through their reflection in the waters. The meadows are enriched with thyme, grasses, daisies, and clover; and the edges of the banks concealed by growths of trees, meadow-sweet, flags, and other water-loving plants. Figures and cattle enliven the scene, but not obtrusively; the design of the sky balancing the weight of the poplar trees, and opposing their direction, from the main theme of the picture.

Alfred East, who was born at Kettering in 1849, was elected an associate of the Royal Academy in 1899. Upon assuming the presidency of the Royal Society of British Artists was created a knight. He studied for awhile in Paris in his youth, but it was a visit to Japan in his mature years that most profoundly affected and developed his art. He died in London in 1913, aged 64.

Jean Honoré Fragonard
1732-1806

ON the sunny Mediterranean, at Grasse, there was born on April 5, 1732, a lad who was to become famous as Jean Honoré Fragonard. His father was a glove-maker of the little town, and for sixteen years the lad lived in his mountain home, and it was probably this garden of France which was to account for his love of trees and flowers all his life. His father made the too-frequent mistake of apprenticing his son to a trade contrary to his inclination and he was put to learn the notary profession.

It was not long before the boy maddened his employer by his constant sketching, upon which his mother determined to take a hand in the matter, and going straight to the famous Boucher, then at the height of his fame in Paris, asked him to teach her son. The kind-hearted Boucher suggested that the boy should return in six months and should go meanwhile to Chardin, that " he might learn to handle his brushes." To Chardin he did go; but made so little progress that Chardin dismissed him, and at the end of six months, he returned to Boucher, who, being pleased with his improvement, kept him.

Having won the Prix de Rome, at 24, which meant that he was entitled to go to Italy for study at the king's expense, he departed with a warning from Boucher that he should not take too seriously the great Italian masters, but follow his own example and remain a Frenchman. If we wish to understand and appreciate the work of Fragonard, Boucher, Watteau, and others of their period, we must not make too close a comparison between them and the great Italians, and we must remember that the Frenchmen were the typical product of their time and country and that, from the artistic point of view to their great credit, they remained Frenchmen, influenced very slightly—if at all—by Italy. After six years' absence, Fragonard returned to his beloved Paris in 1761, and it was not long before his lucky commission came for the painting of " The Swing," from Baron Saint-Julien, a wealthy young courtier.

THE SWING

By JEAN HONORÉ FRAGONARD

In the Wallace Collection—French School

Jean Honoré Fragonard
1732-1806

ON the sunny Mediterranean, at Grasse, there was born on April 5, 1732, a lad who was to become famous as Jean Honoré Fragonard. His father was a glove-maker of the little town, and for sixteen years the lad lived in his mountain home, and it was probably this garden of France which was to account for his love of trees and flowers all his life. His father made the too-frequent mistake of apprenticing his son to a trade contrary to his inclination and he was put to learn the notary profession.

It was not long before the boy maddened his employer by his constant sketching, upon which his mother determined to take a hand in the matter, and going straight to the famous Boucher, then at the height of his fame in Paris, asked him to teach her son. The kind-hearted Boucher suggested that the boy should return in six months and should go meanwhile to Chardin, that " he might learn to handle his brushes." To Chardin he did go; but made so little progress that Chardin dismissed him, and at the end of six months, he returned to Boucher, who, being pleased with his improvement, kept him.

Having won the Prix de Rome, at 24, which meant that he was entitled to go to Italy for study at the king's expense, he departed with a warning from Boucher that he should not take too seriously the great Italian masters, but follow his own example and remain a Frenchman. If we wish to understand and appreciate the work of Fragonard, Boucher, Watteau, and others of their period, we must not make too close a comparison between them and the great Italians, and we must remember that the Frenchmen were the typical product of their time and country and that, from the artistic point of view to their great credit, they remained Frenchmen, influenced very slightly—if at all—by Italy. After six years' absence, Fragonard returned to his beloved Paris in 1761, and it was not long before his lucky commission came for the painting of " The Swing," from Baron Saint-Julien, a wealthy young courtier.

This beautiful composition, the landscape of which was undoubtedly based on the recollection of the Villa d'Este, in Italy, immediately made the painter famous and other commissions showered upon him. He was engaged

(Continued)

THE FAIR-HAIRED BOY

By JEAN HONORÉ FRAGONARD

In the Wallace Collection—French School

for some years on works of this type for rich patrons and also assisted Boucher with many of his important undertakings, as his old master was getting enfeebled and unable to carry out all that was required of him. With the view of helping his former pupil, " his Frago," as he so affectionately called him, Boucher introduced him to his old friend and patron, the wealthy farmer, General Bergeret de Grandcour, who henceforth became Fragonard's best patron and loyal friend until the Revolution parted them.

The arrival from his native town of a young woman called Marie Anne Gérard, sent by her parents to earn her living in Paris, in a shop of a scent seller called Isnard, changed the whole course of Fragonard's career. Marie had a taste for painting fans and Fragonard set about teaching her, and in 1769 they were married. This marriage immediately affected the painter's art, and from the study of frivolous subjects he now took an immense interest in scenes of home-life and domestic happiness, and soon we find beautiful children appearing upon his easel. Among these the Wallace Collection possesses two lovely examples—" The School Mistress " and " The Fair-haired Boy," who was his son, Alexandre Evariste Fragonard, born in 1780, the subject of our colour plate. A child study suited to every time and clime.

We have spoken of Fragonard's period of prosperity under the patronage of rich and powerful clients and of his second period, after his happy marriage when he lived a quieter life surrounded by his devoted family, very different from his former circles; unfortunately, he was to know a third period, one of disillusionment and poverty.

The accession of Louis XVI to the throne of France, at 20 years of age, was the opening chapter of a tragic story of the Revolution, all too well known. Fragonard was to be—at least, financially and socially—one of its victims. In daily fear of being denounced by the Extremists, he contrived to escape from Paris to his native town Grasse, where, with his family, he waited for the storm to abate. On his return to Paris, although he lived on till 1806, to the age of 74, he was quite unable to adapt himself to the art of the period. Nevertheless, he made pitiful attempts to mould his style to conform with the new political ideas, but it was all in vain.

His circumstances became critical, but he was loyally befriended in his great poverty by the painter David, who gratefully remembered past friendships.

DIANA OF THE UPLANDS

By CHARLES WELLINGTON FURSE, A.R.A.

In the Tate Gallery—British School

Charles Wellington Furse, A.R.A.
1868-1905

THE painter of " Diana of the Uplands " was the son of the Archdeacon of Westminster and was born at Halsden House, North Devon, in the year 1868. A handsome, dignified man of great personal charm, his cheerful and cultured manners gave no indication of the malady which was to cut short his life at an early age. Furse married, in 1900, a daughter of John Addington Symonds, the well-known writer, but spent only four years of married life with her. He died on October 17 of the year of his election as an Associate of the Royal Academy.

In his death, at the early age of thirty-seven, England lost a painter of great realistic power. Technically he had something in common with his contemporary, Sargent, and had, indeed, in his short life, mastered the art of painting in a broad and vigorous manner.

He could fill canvases with life-size figures, animals, and a natural and pleasing landscape. " Diana of the Uplands " is not only a dignified portrait, but a composition in which the two greyhounds help to emphasise the youth and beauty of the lady who so firmly, but delicately, holds them in leash. The black of the dog, in the foreground, is admirably contrasted with the white dress of Diana. She is truly a modern counterpart of the classical goddess, and there is nothing incongruous in the fact that she is dressed in the fashion of her time. A very happy and healthy picture; it is full of light and air; there is a wind on the heath, strong and invigorating, which is cleverly rendered.

The picture may be said to symbolise a type of womanhood temporarily eclipsed in Victorian times, but common to all ages; a woman none the less feminine because of her interest in open-air life and sport. She looks confidently towards the spectator, not unaware of her power, not unconscious of her beauty, slightly mysterious, though it is veiled under her large straw hat. She is ready for homage, and none could accord her more intelligent devotion than the artist who looked so successfully with " divining eyes " upon her youth and grace.

MRS. SIDDONS

By THOMAS GAINSBOROUGH, R.A.

In the National Gallery—British School

Thomas Gainsborough, R.A.

1727-1788

THOMAS GAINSBOROUGH, son of John Gainsborough, a wool-stapler, was born at Sudbury, in Suffolk, in 1727, one of a large family. At the local Grammar School, conducted by his uncle, the Reverend Humphrey Burroughs, the lad learnt but little, and at twelve his mind was set on painting, and he was never so happy as when spending the day sketching in the woods. An amusing story is told of this period of his father refusing a letter asking for a day of holiday from school; the boy so cleverly forged the letter that the holiday was secured. All, however, was discovered, upon which the indignant father exclaimed "Tom will be hanged," but, on looking at the sketches, the result of the truant day, he revised his decision and remarked with joy: " No, he will be a genius ! "

After a family meeting, the young painter, for such he was already, was packed off to London and became a pupil of Hayman, a friend of Hogarth. At the age of 17, Gainsborough decided to start for himself, taking lodgings in Hatton Garden, offering his work to dealers. But there being little demand for his pictures, he gave up the struggle and returned, in 1745, to his native Sudbury. Here a chance meeting in the woods with a young and beautiful girl, called Margaret Burr, was one of the important events of his life, for they were married in 1746 and, shortly after, went to live at Ipswich in a house at a rental of six pounds per annum !

Mrs. Gainsborough being endowed not only with good looks, but also with what was then a large income, two hundred pounds a year, the young painter was able to follow his own inclination by painting from nature and only occasionally a portrait. It was during this Ipswich period that Gainsborough produced some of his most beautiful early works, and among them is the picture called " The Painter's Daughters," one of whom is chasing a butterfly, now in the National Gallery, London.

About the year 1758, on the advice of his friend, Philip Thickness, Gainsborough moved from Ipswich to Bath, and lived

(Continued)

there many years where his house, 24 The Circus, may be still seen.

His studio was the meeting place of all the celebrities of the day, and he painted musicians and actors, among the latter being Garrick and Mrs. Siddons. During this Bath period, there was a carrier named Wiltshire who was engaged by Gainsborough to take his pictures to London, and the carrier refusing to accept payment on the ground " that he admired painting too much to make profit by it," Gainsborough, being of a proud disposition, made an arrangement by which he was to be paid in pictures. As it turned out, this was a fortunate arrangement for the carrier's family, for at least one picture appears to have been sold by his grandson for £30,000 !

In 1768, the Royal Academy was founded, and Gainsborough was among the thirty-four names enrolled as original members.

It was probably the great reputation of Reynolds in London that decided Gainsborough to try his fortune there. So it fell out that, in 1774, he packed all his belongings, his paintings, drawings and endless musical instruments in the waggon of Mr. Wiltshire and the journey to London was made : the painter travelling in the Bath Coach.

From the outset, Gainsborough was a great success and very soon he became a rival to the great Sir Joshua Reynolds, and between the two, for many years, there was no great friendship. In all probability these strained relations were due to Gainsborough's disposition, for he was proud and short tempered, which, more than once, lead to disagreeable incidents with his patrons.

A word must be said as to Gainsborough's gifts as a landscape painter, in which art he outshone Reynolds entirely. It is this ability to paint landscapes which makes some of his early portraits in landscapes so fascinating.

His famous work " The Market Cart," in the National Gallery, is a magnificent study of English countryside. We reproduce here important works of this great painter, all of them favourites of the public.

The majestic " Portrait of Mrs. Siddons," was painted during the Bath period, and represents the famous actress at the age of 39, in powdered wig and make up. It is one of the finest portraits of the period possessed by the National Gallery.

" The Blue Boy " is a portrait of Master Jonathan Buttall, and was till

(Continued)

recent years in the collection of the Duke of Westminster, when it was sold for a fabulous sum, probably the largest amount ever paid for an old painting; it is now in the celebrated Huntingdon collection, in the United States. The picture is said to have been painted as a challenge to Sir Joshua Reynolds, who had declared, in one of his discourses, that a mass of blue in a painting was impossible, and the result, it will be generally agreed, proved that Reynolds, as an art critic, was not so great as Reynolds the painter, and it shows also the danger of the favourite pastime of some critics of inventing theories to fit all artists.

One of the most exquisite portraits by Gainsborough is that of the Hon. Mrs. Graham, in the National Gallery of Scotland. The lady died soon after the portrait was painted, at the age of 35, when her husband, then Lord Lynedoch, being so greatly distressed at his loss, and unable to bear the view of the portrait, had it bricked up in his London house. The later history of this work is interesting, as it was left by will, many years afterwards, by a relation of the husband to the " National Gallery " and was claimed, accordingly, by the London National Gallery. As, however, it was discovered, by the terms of the will, that the picture was never to leave Scotland, it was obvious that it was meant for Edinburgh, where it has remained ever since.

A reference has already been made to Gainsborough's musical instruments of which he had a large collection of every conceivable kind. His passion for collecting violins, flutes, and indeed every kind of instrument was not equalled by his skill in performing on them—although he took no small pride in his musical achievements. There are amusing stories told of him in this connection; one of which is that, hearing of a double-bass instrument in the possession of a musical teacher, he called upon him and peremptorily asked the price. Having bought the instrument, after a hard bargain, he then insisted on carrying away a book of music and finally required the musician to come himself the same day to start teaching him.

Thomas Gainsborough lived but 61 years, for, after a period of suffering, he died on August 2, 1788. Feeling that his end was near, he wrote to Reynolds, seeking a reconciliation, to which Sir Joshua responded immediately. It is said, as Reynolds left the room, Gainsborough bade him goodbye, adding " We are going to Heaven and Van Dyck is of the company."

THE BROKEN PITCHER
By JEAN-BAPTISTE GREUZE
In the Louvre—French School

Jean-Baptiste Greuze
1725-1805

THERE are few artists who enjoyed and endured the changing caprice of fortune more than Jean-Baptiste Greuze. He was the son of a builder and was born in the reign of Louis XV, at Tournus, near Macon. Apprenticed to a painter at Lyons, he acquired a ready technique, and, when he arrived in Paris at the age of thirty, he was equipped to exploit the dawning fashion, sponsored to some extent by Rousseau, of idealising the beauty and morality of peasant-life. His first success at the Salon was the picture entitled " Father of a Family reading the Bible to his Children."

Greuze came under the protection of an Abbé of influence and, travelling with him to Rome, he entered into the social life and made a study of the art of the Eternal City. He also fell in love with an Italian countess, one of his pupils. For some reason she was unable to marry him, but Greuze consoled himself by taking as his wife the beautiful daughter of a Parisian bookseller. She inspired him with a long series of pictures of which " The Broken Pitcher " and " The Milkmaid " are typical examples. But she was anything but the sweet and gentle creature depicted in his canvases. Her caprice and immodesty made the painter's life unbearable, if we believe Greuze's pathetic confession of his domestic troubles published in the De Goncourt's book on eighteenth-century French artists.

In 1761, Greuze moved Paris to enthusiasm by his most famous work, " The Village Bride." When the Salon opened that year, the picture was not ready, and although Greuze made a great effort to hurry it, the canvas arrived only six days before the exhibition closed. It was everywhere acclaimed, and found in Diderot a powerful champion, since the great critic professed to see in it the full realisation of his own moral principles of art.

Greuze made immense sums of money out of his pictures and engravings from them, but he incurred the jealousy and disfavour of the Academicians, who refused to allow him to exhibit again in the Salon until he had painted what might be called his " diploma " work, required of every Academician.

The fact is that Greuze was intensely vain and could brook neither the

(Continued)

THE MILKMAID

By JEAN-BAPTISTE GREUZE

In the Louvre—French School

rules of the Academy nor criticism. However, he did at last paint an historical subject, the condition of his election. The Members assembled, but would accept him only as a subject painter. The president adding " Your early work was excellent, the Academy must close its eyes to this one." Greuze was staggered and attempted to convince the Academicians of the merit of this historical picture. They merely laughed at his expostulations. Angered by what he considered a slight to his genius, Greuze withdrew from the Salon and held exhibitions in his own studio at the Louvre, which became the haunt of the fashionable and intellectual world. It was the show place of Paris.

Meanwhile, the Revolution, which was to engulf not only the aristocrats, but nearly all those who were supported by the old régime, darkened the horizon of the painter's life, and, when the storm burst in full fury, Greuze found himself a ruined man. From fame and riches he had sunk, at the age of 76, to such poverty and despair that he wrote to the Minister of Interior that he had lost everything, " even his courage and talent." He died at the age of 80, a disillusioned man. But for him Death had no terror. "I am ready for the journey," he said to his friend, Barthelemy, before he died. "Good-bye, you will be alone at my funeral, like the beggar's dog." Two mourners followed him when he was buried and a weeping woman placed a wreath of immortelles on his coffin, as he passed by, with these words : " These flowers, offered by the most grateful of his pupils, are the emblems of his glory." It is an interesting fact that "The Broken Pitcher " was one of the prized possessions of Madame du Barry, and when her effects were nationalised during the Revolution it became State property.

The popularity of Greuze's pictures, however, revived in the nineteenth century. They combine a certain elegance with simplicity. Having invented a style that gratified public taste, he merely sought to repeat his successes.

It was his fate to be born in a somewhat trivial and corrupt time; it was his misfortune to be old and fixed in his ideas when the Revolution demanded young men and new methods. It is related that this once all-successful painter received a commission at the age of 78 to paint a portrait of Napoleon, but the Emperor, who disliked sittings to artists, merely gave permission to Greuze to look at him for a few minutes. This was one of Greuze's last works.

Arthur Hacker, R.A.

1859-1919

OF what is she thinking, this young mother, as she sits with hands clasped, gazing at her first-born cushioned upon the floor? Is there any anxiety or doubt—doubt about her husband, or anxiety for her child's future? The artist has hidden her face, a mask of discreet shadow providing a pretty little enigma for us. The clock ticks upon the wall, signalling the hour when her good man may be expected. Clearly he is a fisherman; the nets and lobster-pot indicate his calling. Though poverty is here, the home is not necessarily wretched. The plump, dimpled arms of the young mother tell their own tale, and the hardships of life have not yet impaired her comeliness. She has been mending a fishing net, and baby himself is partly swathed in the net which hangs before the fireplace. A few flowers lie upon the footstool and one solitary bloom is clutched in the infant's hand.

Such a subject as this was the theme of many young artists during the last two decades of the nineteenth century. By their very homeliness, pictures of village life—and especially of fishing villages and fisher-folk—were sure of a popular welcome. Sentiment was regarded as a laudable human attribute. It is evident here that it was the painter's intention by a display of technique, although Arthur Hacker's brushwork could be extremely dexterous.

It has often been said that a picture should not be divided into two completely equivalent halves, yet, in this case, so cleverly has this rule been broken that the observer would hardly be conscious of it unless directed to it. Yet no one can fail to note that the distribution of interest, of light and shade and of balance of forms, are completely successful. This has been achieved by the well-judged arrangement of those shapes which take the light.

" The Young Mother " was painted in 1889, when the artist was 30 years old. He was born in London, the son of an engraver, and after a period of study at the Royal Academy Schools, went to Paris and entered the atelier of Bonnat, whose methods he assimilated to a large degree. Later, he visited Morocco, Algiers, Spain, and Italy. He died very suddenly in London in 1919.

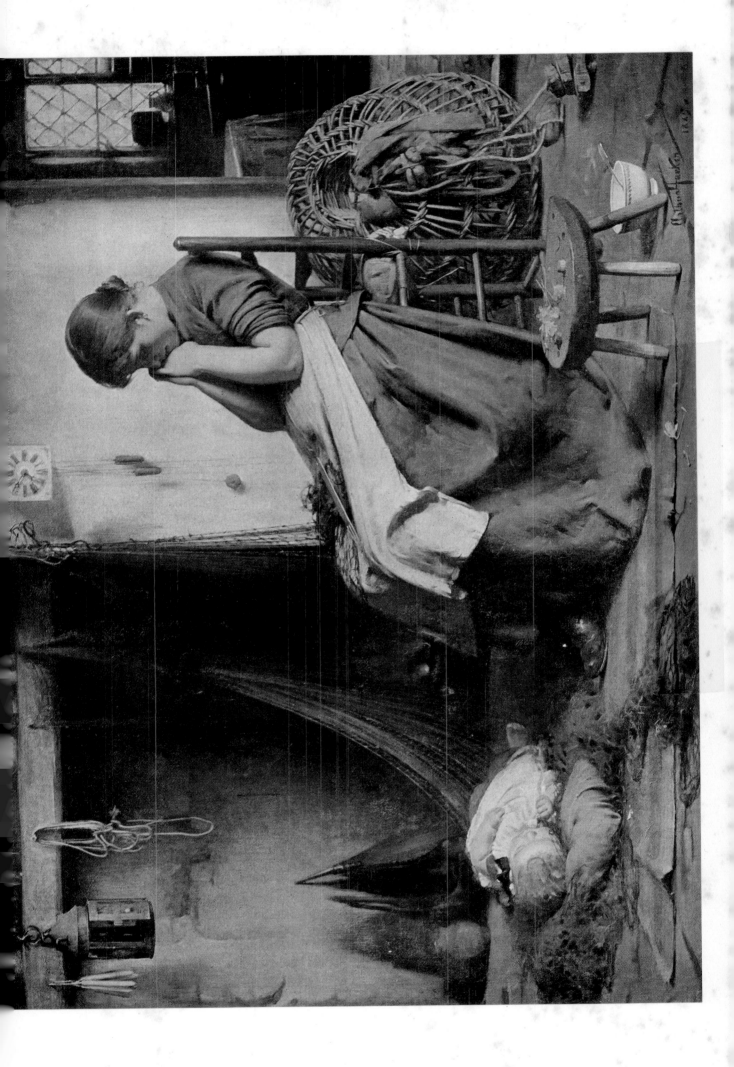

Henry Holiday
1839-1927

HENRY HOLIDAY began early in his life to paint subjects from Dante, whose works he had read in translations before he was nineteen. He had tried his wings upon various small pictures and illustrations from the *Vita Nuova* and the *Divina Comedia* many years before he attempted his most celebrated, and certainly most popular, work, " Dante and Beatrice." None of them, however, had anything of a reception; and, feeling that something was wanting, the artist set out for Florence in the autumn of 1881, earnest in the endeavour to recapture the spirit and to realise something of the appearance of Dante's city.

As the setting of his subject, he chose a spot at the end of Ponte Trinita, looking towards the Ponte Vecchio with San Miniato in the distance. After deciding upon this, he proceeded to study Italian pictures of the thirteenth and fourteenth centuries for details of buildings, searching also among archives of the city. In a back street he discovered a remnant of an old herring-bone pavement which appears in the picture. On his return to London, he made clay models in the nude for the figures of Beatrice and Monna Vanna, her companion, afterwards clothing them in draperies ; he even made clay models of the old houses on the Arno from which to paint.

The picture was shown at Grosvenor Gallery before it was quite completed, and after the exhibition Henry Holiday finished it, his friend, Nettleship, adding the pigeons in the road. The following year it was sent to the Liverpool annual exhibition. It was there purchased by an admirer, who presented it to the Walker Art Gallery. The story of the picture is told by the artist. " Dante had confided to a friend his devotion to Beatrice and as he was in consequence much in her society, many thought he was courting her. Since he did not wish his affection for Beatrice to be known, he allowed the belief to go uncontradicted; so that when the lady left Florence and Dante did not follow her, or show signs of grief at her absence, the gossips thought he was playing fast and loose. The report of this reached Beatrice, who, at their next meeting, passed him and denied him her " divine salutation."

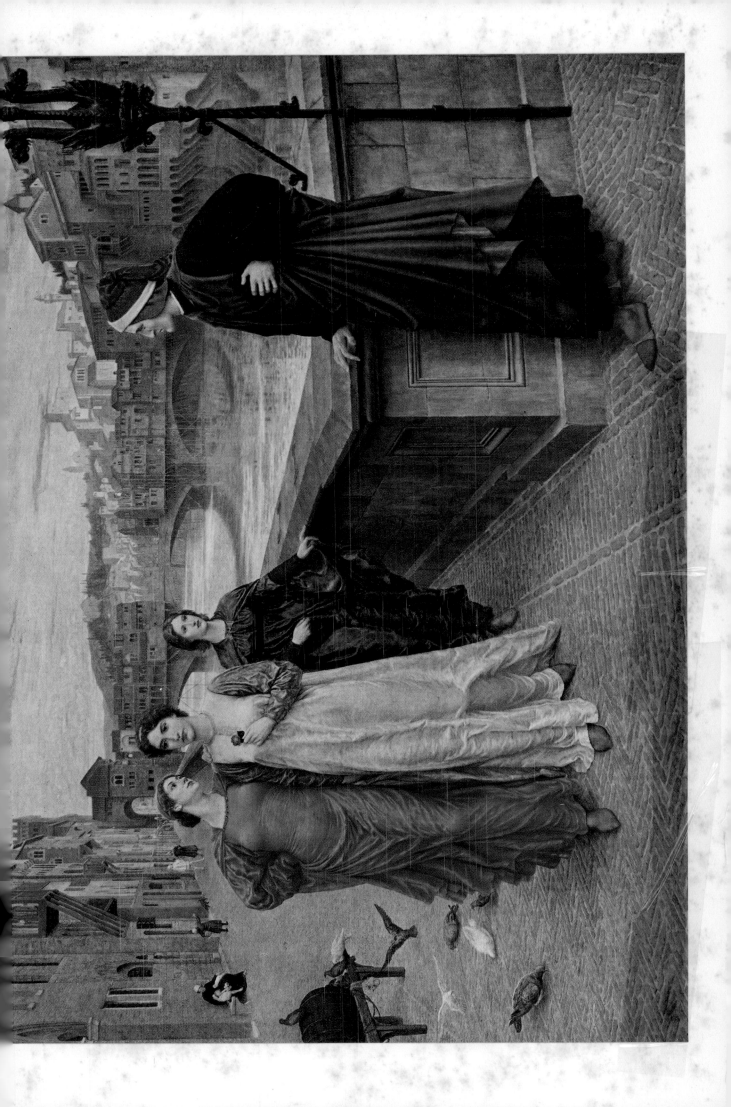